Hello Happiness

175 Inspirations
to Brighten Up Your Day

Robert Holden

Hodder & Stoughton

Copyright © 1999 by Robert Holden

First published in Great Britain in 1999 by Hodder and Stoughton
A division of Hodder Headline PLC

The right of Robert Holden to be identified as the Author of the Work
has been asserted by him in accordance with the Copyright, Designs
and Patents Act 1988.

1   3   5   7   9   8   6   4   2

British Library Cataloguing in Publication Data
A CIP Catalogue record for this title is available from the British Library

ISBN 0 340 75065 0

Printed and bound in Great Britain by
Caledonian International Book Manufacturing Ltd, Glasgow

Hodder and Stoughton
A division of Hodder Headline PLC
338 Euston Road
London NW1 3BH

To Tom and Linda Carpenter

Acknowledgements

My sincere thanks go to my wife, Miranda Holden, to my brother, David Holden, and to the team of The Happiness Project, in particular, Ben Renshaw, Candy Constable and Alison Atwell. I would also like to thank Anne Burkett, for your great support. Thank you to everyone who dares to love and be happy.

You who chase happiness so incessantly,
give up the chase. Stop awhile, and let
happiness chase after you.

Slow down awhile, cease to hurry
for a moment, and let the inner happiness
bubble up.

Try not to think of happiness as something external that travels to you or away from you, but think of happiness as a potential you carry within you always – a potential you are, in any given moment, either opening to or withdrawing from.

The *pursuit of happiness* must always fail because it is based on a lie – happiness is not outside you. Until you change your belief that happiness is somewhere else, you will never quite make it!

The gift of happiness is wrapped in your heart, not in the world outside. Your happiness will never be mailed to you, and it can never get lost in the post! In truth, your happiness has already been delivered, and it is sitting in your inner mail box – your heart – waiting to be opened.

The source of all your fears stems from a single erroneous belief, *happiness is somewhere else*.

The soul is JOY!

Happiness is not in things; happiness is in you.

E.G.O. is the fearful belief that
*E*verything *G*ood's *O*utside.
True happiness is transcendental – it is
beyond ego.

The greatest pain of all is the fear that
happiness might somehow elude you for ever;
the greatest joy of all is the realisation that
the potential for happiness is available to
you now and always.

A man and a woman travelled the world
in search of happiness. They finally discovered
that true happiness has no destination;
rather, it is a way of travelling.

Happiness is not a search; it's a choice.

Happiness is only ever one thought away – at most! One fresh perception, one new belief, one powerful decision is all it takes to experience a world of difference.

Happinessisnowhere!

The only difference between 'happiness is no where' and 'happiness is now here' is not the event, but how you see the event. Perception is the key.

Happiness is all about milking the 'sacred NOW'.

In the English language, the word 'present' has three distinct meanings: 'here', 'now' and 'a gift'. Truly, the greatest gifts are always available to you here and now!

Tombstone: Here lies a man died at twenty, buried at forty. He died long before his death. His happiness was short-lived for he was too busy building a glorious future.

You will never *become* happy – you can
only *be* happy.

Speak to any true spiritual teacher or guru
worth their mantra, so to speak, and they will
tell you that NOW is sacred. Therefore, make
sure you are living in the NOW.
If you want happiness, it is important not
to *futurise* or *pasturise* too much!

Let's make today one of the good old days!

How much happiness can you handle today?
How much happiness will you allow yourself?

I have a friend who calls his alarm clock
an 'opportunity clock'. It is his way of
reminding himself that today will present as
many opportunities for life, love and
laughter as he is prepared to see.

There once was a man who waited all his life
to be happy. The last anyone heard of him, he
was still waiting. To be happy you have to
lose the WAIT PROBLEM!

Whilst you wait, happiness waits.
Whilst you wait, love waits.
Whilst you wait, peace waits.
Whilst you wait, freedom waits.
Whilst you wait, opportunity waits.
Whilst you wait, the world waits.
Whilst you wait, we all wait.

Life is all about *being first!*
If you want love, be loving first;
if you want trust, be trusting first;
if you want forgiveness, be forgiving first;
if you want honesty, be honest first;
if you want courage, be courageous first;
if you want inspiration, be a Light first!

Happiness cannot happen without your decision
   to be happy.
Love cannot grow without your decision
   to be loving.
Peace cannot blossom without your decision
   to be peaceful.
Freedom cannot bloom without your decision
   to be free.
Miracles cannot flower without your decision
   to be open.
Bliss cannot flourish without your decision
   to be guiltless.
Heaven cannot bear its fruits without your decision
   to receive.

If you want to be happy – the *youniverse* is on
   your side.
If you want to be successful – the *youniverse* is
   here to help.
If you want to love – the *youniverse* will assist
   you.
If you want to live – the *youniverse* can
   accommodate that.
If you want to sing – the *youniverse* can
   organise it.
In fact, whatever you want, all you have to do
   is want it, and your *youniverse* will arrange it.

The #1 Happiness Principle is:

Unless you are happy with yourself, you will
   not be happy with what you do;
Unless you are happy with yourself, you will
   not be happy with what you have;
Unless you are happy with yourself, you will
   not be happy with where you are;
Unless you are happy with yourself, you will
   not be happy with who you are with.

You will accept as much happiness, love
and peace as you think you deserve. Any more
and you must choose either to,
1) sabotage and push away your joy, or,
2) change your mind about yourself.

The belief that *happiness has to be deserved* has
led to centuries of pain, guilt and deception.

Happiness is free – there are no conditions.

Can there ever be such a thing as a free lunch?
Well, it all depends where you go to eat.
A blue sky is free. The moon is free.
The mountains are free. The river is free.
Joy is free. Love is free. A smile is free.
Laughter is free.

You do not *deserve* happiness,
you *choose* happiness. Happiness is natural.
It is freely available to all. It is unconditional.
And when you too are unconditional about
happiness, then happiness merely happens.

Do you deserve your left leg?
Do you deserve your right ear?
Do you deserve your nostrils? Of course not!
They are given to you. It is the same with
happiness. Happiness is not deserved,
earned or won. Happiness is given,
and it is given to enjoy.

There once was a man who suffered diligently all his life in order to buy a single moment of pure happiness. One day he packed all of his suffering into a big heavy bag, slung it over his shoulder and headed to market. When he tried to trade in his suffering, he was told there is no exchange rate between suffering and happiness. In other words, suffering cannot buy happiness.

When you try to play the martyr, you lose
and so does everyone else.
Your giving becomes more and more
conditional, full of hidden emotional
invoices that must be returned within
twenty-eight days,
hours,
minutes,
seconds . . .

There once was a monk who meditated
alone in a cave for forty years.
He owned nothing. He ate nothing.
He drank water. He could walk on water.
He could recite any sacred scripture.
He could stand on his head for hours.
He could see auras. In spite of all these years of
sacrifice, he was still bloody miserable for he
had yet to learn how to love and be happy.

Happiness requires no sacrifice,
only acceptance.

You can double and multiply your own
personal joy every time you let yourself be
pleased for another person's good fortune.
Some Buddhists refer to this skill as
'sympathetic joy'.

'I am doing a lot of work on myself,' said my client.

'Do you ever tire of working so hard on yourself?' I asked.

'What do you mean?'

'Well, maybe all this hard work is somehow holding you back. Why not give up working so hard at self-improvement and see what a little self-acceptance does for you. In other words, *give yourself a break.*'

'You mean no more hard work,' she said.

'Yes – only self-acceptance,' I said.

'I'll work on it,' she said.

Has it ever occurred to you that you might be
trying too hard to be happy?

Happiness happens when you let it.

Choose peace. Give up the fight.
Let go of the belief that there must always be
an enemy or a war somewhere in your life.

That which you try to control withers, fades
and dies. Have you ever noticed that the people
you succeed in controlling appear less attractive
to you after a while? You cannot be in control
and happy. Lose control – and be happy!

Affirm to yourself: 'Just for today I will not struggle. Every time I am tempted to struggle, I will smile. And then I will pray for peace.'

Let today be a day of blessings. Bless the sun.
Bless your breakfast. Bless the traffic.
Bless your boss. Bless your coffee.
Bless all your phone-calls and e-mails.
Bless your family. Bless the dog.
Bless your evening meal. Bless everything.
This is how to feel blessed.

The world is feedback. In every given moment the world is feeding back to you your state of mind. The world is a mind-mirror. Therefore, if you want a great day, think great thoughts.

If you want to remember today for ever, tell at least ten people 'I love you'. Years later, this will make a great bar story, or a good tale to tell the grandchildren.

Take time today to write a list of every
significant person in your life.
Then picture each person, one at a time,
and out loud dedicate your relationship
with them to total love. This process may
take one or two hours, but the benefits
will last for ever.

I once asked a dying man if he had any regrets.
'Only that I did not appreciate all that I had
a little sooner,' he said.

Dear God.
I declare today a day of Amnesty in which
I gratefully volunteer to hand over all of my
resentments and grievances to You.
Please help me to handle well all of the
peace that must inevitably follow.
Amen.

Pain is the result of holding on to a
negative thought about yourself; joy comes
from accepting only loving thoughts.
Let go now and be healed.

There comes a moment in everyone's life when they must choose between resentment and joy. Resentment will poison the carrier, chain you to your past and make your perception bitter and twisted. Letting the resentment go is your first step to freedom. This is the most perfect revenge, for now you can be truly happy.

Resentment costs too much.
Make no mistake, it is you who has to pay
the bill for the resentment you hold on to.
It is your nervous system, your lungs, your
muscles, your heart, your perception and
your mind that deteriorate and decay
every moment you try to defend
yourself with hate.

When you forgive anyone – it sets you free.

Forgiveness is the choice for wholeness.
It is the medium of miracles.
Through forgiveness you affirm,
1) I am whole;
2) no one can threaten or take away
my wholeness.

To forgive, love must mean more to
you than pain.

The moment you imprison anyone
you become a jailer. Now you have a new
job – a new pre*occupation* – and now
you are both doing time.

Sometimes in order to be happy in the present moment you have to be willing to give up all hope of a better past.

The highest truth about your past is that it is passed. So what are you up to now? Are you re-playing the video of your awful past – a horror story you frighten yourself with over and over – or are you ready for a new story, a love story, a success story, a story of freedom from fear, and victory over the past?

True happiness is a permanent inner smile
that is gloriously unaffected by the look
of outward things.

Happiness is a great big 'let go'!

Gratitude is open heart therapy.

Before we practise gratitude, we are in
the dark and there appears very little to be
grateful for. Once we begin to practise
gratitude, a new light dawns, sometimes
a brilliant light, a light as bright
as heaven itself.

When you decide with all your heart
to look for happiness, happiness finds you.
It is the same with love.
It is the same with everything.

To whom are you grateful in your life?
Do these people know the full extent of
your gratitude? Do you realise how grateful
they will be when you tell them?

Real wealth is not about how much
you have, but about how much you
appreciate what you have. This is because
real wealth is an 'estate of mind'.

If you want to be happy – money helps.
If you want to be miserable – money helps.
If you want to be generous – money helps.
If you want to be miserly – money helps.
If you want to be free – money helps.
If you want to dig a pit – money helps.
If you want to go to heaven – money helps.
If you want to go to hell – money helps.

Nothing in the world can make you happy;
everything in the world can encourage
you to be happy.
Nothing in the world can make you sad;
everything in the world can encourage
you to be sad.

More 'stuff' cannot buy you more happiness.

It's so unfair – people who are grateful always
seem to have something to be happy about!

Whatever you appreciate, appreciates in value.

Give compliments today.
Compliment and encourage everyone today.
Make a point of recognising all the qualities,
strengths and characteristics you aspire
to in every person you meet.
This is the key to self-realisation.

Today, decide *to be* what you want.
If you want love, be loving.
If you want honesty, be honest.
If you want friendship, be friendly.
If you want encouragement, be encouraging.
If you want forgiveness, be forgiving.
Be what you want!

Your ego says 'give as good as you get';
your spirit says 'you get as good as you give'.
One is a philosophy of fear; the other
a philosophy of love.

Practise generosity today – be surprisingly
generous today.

Has it ever occurred to you that what you feel
you are not currently getting – from someone,
something or somewhere – might be exactly
what you are not giving?

If you are looking for happiness and you
can't find any, maybe you are suffering from
too much 'I strain'.

The more you give to NOW,
the more you get from NOW!

There are not shortages, only a lack of
willingness to receive.

Gratitude is more than an attitude;
gratitude is a philosophy. The philosophy of
gratitude begins as a hope, grows into a belief,
and finally becomes an absolute knowing.
It is a knowing that within any given situation
– peaceful or painful, beautiful or ugly –
there is always a gift waiting,
wanting you to see it.

No matter how hard you try it is impossible
to be grateful and depressed.

Any resistance you may be experiencing to
practising unconditional gratitude is really a
desire to hold on to pain or a fear of joy.

'The Way to Heaven'
How to get from 'here' to 'there'.
Step One: There are no steps.
Step Two: Heaven is *here* already.
Step Three: So are you.
Step Four: You must be *there* by now.

Happiness requires no next step;
it is already here!

Practise wonder today – be present,
begin again, know nothing, and allow
everything to surprise you, inspire you,
excite you, entertain you, teach you.
Be fully open to life, today,
and let yourself live wonder-fully.

There once was a pessimist who wandered
through heaven, convinced he was in hell.
'I knew there wasn't a heaven,' he muttered.
We see what we believe.

Cynics and optimists continue to argue
with each other about who is right and who is
being realistic. The truth is, the cynic is right.
The cynic sees exactly what he wants to see;
his world is very real to him. The optimist is
also right. The optimist sees exactly what he
wants to see; his world is very real to him.
They are both right – they are both making
their own reality.

Be honest – have you ever seen a cynical baby?
Have you ever stared into a cot, held a baby's
hand and whispered lovingly, 'You're so sweet
and cynical'? No? There are no cynical babies!
You are not born cynical. You do not just
become cynical. You choose cynicism.
You use cynicism to protect and defend
against getting hurt ever again. You will
get hurt, however, because you can't
be cynical and happy.

One man's garden was full of weeds.
Another man's garden was full of flowers.
Both gardens were full of daisies.

If it appears you have nothing to be
grateful for, it is because you are not allowing
yourself to receive. Just because you do not
receive does not mean there is nothing to
receive. On the contrary, there is always
something to receive, and so there is always a
reason to be grateful. Pray, 'Dear God, teach
me I am worthy to receive, teach me
how to receive, teach me gratitude.'

**Although I have never actually seen a lump
of happiness, I suspect it is heart-shaped.**

Love and be happy.

First love, then think.
First love, then speak.
First love, then look.
First love, then choose.
First love, then give.
First love, then act.
First love, then teach.
First love, then be.

Know Love; no fear.

Know Joy; no pain.

Know Light; no darkness.

Know Wholeness; no dis-ease.

Know Now; no past.

Know Truth; no lies.

Know God; no separation.

Know Self; no other.

You do not stop loving because you get afraid;
you get afraid because you stop loving.
You do not stop laughing because you get old;
you get old because you stop laughing.
You do not stop living because you get hurt;
you get hurt because you stop living.

No flower; no fragrance.
No sun; no light.
No air; no life.
No faith; no courage.
No truth; no freedom.
No love; no happiness.

Happiness is not something you have in
your hands or your pockets; happiness is
something you carry in your heart.

Happiness starts with love;
sadness ends with love.

Where there is love,
pain breathes,
tears smile,
hurt softens,
guilt loses its edge,
judgement forgets to judge,
fear is no longer afraid,
separation is over.

Where there is love,
You are there.

To be happy, love must mean more
to you than anything.

Love,
And you will enjoy abundance;
Love,
And you will enjoy success.
Love,
And you will enjoy peace;
Love,
And you will enjoy happiness.
Love,
Place love above everything.
Love,
And you will enjoy everything.

True happiness is what happens when you
come face to face with fear and choose love.

Any unhappiness you experience is
a call for love.

Blessed are they who can smile at themselves,
for they will never cease to be amused.

When life is difficult, be easy on yourself.

You are precious.
Make some time for yourself today.

Unhappiness is not a sin – it is an opportunity
to be truthful and to heal.

All too often we refuse to let go of our fears
until we can see hope; but we cannot see hope
until we are first willing to let go of our fears.

Happiness is not just the absence of sadness,
it is also the capacity to love and
heal your sadness.

Feel your feelings! A feeling has only
one ambition in life and that is to be felt!
You cannot be honestly happy and untruthful
about your sadness.

Healing is not a war; it is a peace process.
It is not about resistance; it is about acceptance.
Acceptance is the key to peace,
love and healing.

In all my years of psychotherapy, I have never had a client who suffered from being too kind to themselves.

Stay open all hours for miracles.

When in fear, feel fear, and commit to love.

When in tears, cry tears, and commit to healing.

When unhappy, honour it, and commit to joy.

When in conflict, own it, and commit to peace.

When in pain, express it, and commit to
freedom.

When angry, feel it, and commit to harmony.

When resentful, be honest, and commit to
forgiveness.

When hurting, nurse yourself, and commit to
laughter.

When down and out, rest up, and commit to
success.

Without acceptance, anger will enrage you.

Without acceptance, guilt will shame you.

Without acceptance, judgement will condemn you.

Without acceptance, anxiety will torment you.

Without acceptance, sadness will depress you.

Without acceptance, fear will terrify you.

Without acceptance, pain will hurt you.

Without acceptance, loneliness will isolate you.

Without acceptance, love cannot love you.

When you are low, get help.
When you are down, get help.
When you are depressed, get help.
When you are bitter, get help.
When you are tired, get help.
When you are tempted to live life
all by yourself, get help.

Today is a good opportunity to practise being less independent. After all, do you want to be independent or happy?

If you are unhappy, maybe it is because you have abandoned your greatest source of strength.

To be happy, it is important to make your peace with God. To some, God is a fiction, a tyrant, an expletive, an aloof dictator, a heartless landlord, a cruel bully who fixes wars and football games. This is not the God I am speaking of. The God I know is a pure, unconditional love, and this powerful, heavenly love is available to all who make themselves available to It.

'Oh Master, how long does it take to be enlightened?' asked the student.

'You guess,' replied the Master.

'Thirty years, maybe?'

'You're right,' said the Master.

'I was going to say forty years, Master,' said another student.

'You're right,' said the Master.

'I was going to say ten years, Master,' said another student.

'You're right,' said the Master.

Pain runs deep; but joy runs even deeper.

Without Self-acceptance, peace is impossible;
with Self-acceptance, peace is yours.
Without Self-acceptance, love has to wait;
with Self-acceptance, love is made welcome.
Without Self-acceptance, there is no happiness;
with Self-acceptance, you know happiness.
Without Self-acceptance, truth hurts;
with Self-acceptance, truth heals.

Just like the ugly duckling, we are afraid
we are not good enough, wrong, bad, and
nothing, and just like the ugly duckling,
we will eventually learn this is not true.

Happiness is innate. It is natural.
It is your core. By contrast, unhappiness is
learned. It is acquired. It is an outer skin
you can grow out of.

You are happy 100 percent of the time.
Happiness is constant, it does not come and go.
What comes and goes is your attunement
to happiness.

True happiness is like an inner light that
has no 'off' switch.

Happiness is good for you – it makes
your skin glow. Laughter is a tonic that
exercises the lungs. A smile is the ultimate
face-lift. Love is known to be good for the
heart. These natural cosmetics can be safely
tested on animals and humans.

Happiness is attractive. Once you decide
to be happy you attract great things into your
life. Your decision to be happy helps you to
radiate and glow. You light up the
world when you are happy.

Could you ever be unreasonably kind
to someone i.e. be kind to someone for
no reason at all?
Could you ever be unreasonably loving
i.e. love someone for no reason?
And could you ever be unreasonably
happy and unreasonably peaceful and
unreasonably generous?
If so, you are an unreasonable fool,
who has found freedom!

We wonder in awe at the young baby who smiles for no reason at all; it is one of life's most beautiful pictures. However, when we see an adult smiling for no reason at all we immediately worry for their mental health. Whoever said happiness needs a reason?

Make yourself available to happiness, and happiness must make itself available to you. Happiness is freely available to us all on a 24-hour 'Don't pay now, don't pay later' basis.

A very telling measure of how confused
we have become about happiness is the extent
to which we use the language of pain to
describe our joy. We say, for instance, 'It was
terribly good', 'It went frightfully well', 'They
were awfully nice', 'It was to die for', 'We got
on like a house on fire', and 'I had a hell
of a time'. Teach yourself happiness requires
no pain down-payments. Happiness is
not a struggle; it's a choice.

Gratitude is good medicine.
One single serving of gratitude is often
enough to open the heart, energise the body,
warm the bones, make your hair curl, put a
spring in your step, start you humming,
and make you smile like a baby!

Smile – it triggers curiosity!

You cannot think your way to happiness.
Happiness is not a formula of thought.
If anything, happiness is the relinquishment
of thoughts, theories and theses.

Happiness happens when you least inspect it.

There once was a cat who chased her tail
round and round. Although she could not quite
catch it, it continued to follow her round.
It is the same with humans and happiness.

What if you were to stop searching for
happiness – and what if you found
it was already here?

There is a world of difference between
searching for happiness and choosing
to be happy.

Remember, happiness is a choice.

You did not come to add to the madness
of this world, you came to be free.
And you did not come empty, for you are
full of gifts to give. Therefore, do not
hide your light – let it shine.
Do not hold back on love – let it flow.
Do not temper your joy – let it inspire.
Do not deny your truth – let it be.
Do not imprison your imagination – set it free.
Do not reign in your creativity – let it go.
Do not mask your playfulness – let it out.
Do not resist your spirit – let it live.

Scatter joy wherever you go.

Right now, are you being real?
Or are you suffering from 'I amnesia'?
Have you forgotten who you are?
Have you forgotten how to be real?
You cannot be unreal and really happy.

Joy is self-acceptance – it is freedom from self-judgement and the need to self-improve. Indeed, no amount of self-improvement can make up for a lack of self-acceptance.

No one can love you more than you are prepared to love yourself and get away with it.

Right in the middle of 'life' is an 'if' –
'I'd be happy if . . .',
'I'd live more if . . .',
'I'll be more loving if . . .',
'I'll be courageous if . . .',
'I'd be honest if . . .'
Stop '*if*-ing' around
and get on with your life.

There are two doors in front of you.
One door says 'Heaven',
the other says 'Lecture on Heaven'.
You must choose between the two doors.
What are you feeling?
What is your choice?

In H.E.A.V.E.N. all the letters stand together:
*H*appiness next to *E*ternity; *A*bundance,
*V*ision and *E*ase joined to *N*ow, as one.

In H.E.L.L. all the letters stand alone:
the *H*orrific *E*ffect of not enough *L*ove
and *L*aughter, waiting to be undone.

Love is heaven. Fear is hell.

Fear, without judgement, is Love.
Anger, without judgement, is Love.
Guilt, without judgement, is Love.
Depression, without judgement, is Love.
Jealousy, without judgement, is Love.
Hate, without judgement, is Love.
Anxiety, without judgement, is Love.
Sadness, without judgement, is Love.
Pain, without judgement, is Love.
Love, without judgement, is Love.

Today is a good day for forgiveness.
Mind you, forgiveness is not for everyone.
It is only for those who would like to
experience peace, love, joy, bliss,
healing, freedom, total salvation
and things like that.

Gratitude is nutrition for the mind – like a
mental multi-vitamin tablet! Take gratitude
daily for a healthy frame of mind full of
perspective, hope, faith, inspiration and
a trust in the perfection of all things.

If you are afraid you may never find the
key to happiness, fear not. There is no lock.
You need no key. Happiness is a sliding door.
As you approach and get close, the doors slide
open automatically for you.

If you are too busy to be happy,
you are too busy!

When you catch yourself living life fast,
it's important you hold on fast to
what's important.

Once a day, every day, 'stop' the world
for just a moment and ask yourself,
'What's important?'
Once you've remembered,
press 'play' again.

The only way to get to happiness is
to be there already!

There once was a farmer who dreamed
ardently of a bumper summer harvest.
He became so preoccupied with his dream
that he forgot to sow any seeds.
Totally distraught, he tried to blame the
field for not producing a crop, and also
his tools, the weather, the government
and God. You have to participate
in your own dream.

If you want to be happy,
be a friend.

The fear that happiness at work leads
to complacency is worth a laugh or two.
Happiness actually inspires confidence,
capacity and creativity. Happiness at work
makes sustainable success possible.

Memo to all managers:
catch people enjoying their work.
A happy team will be more inspired,
dedicated, lively, energetic, creative, friendly
and stress-proofed than any miserable bunch,
no matter how talented.

Work is a state of mind. So is play.

Wisdom is the power of maximising the enjoyment of the present moment.

The world is full of people saving for a rainy day. You would think, then, that rain should bring out the best in everyone. But how many people do you see really enjoying themselves when it rains?

It is never too late to enjoy the moment.

Time is no obstacle to happiness – it takes
as much time to be happy as it does
to be miserable.

True happiness is unselfish.
You cannot contain it, control it, or keep it in.
The first impulse of happiness is you want to
share it. It is impossible to be so happy that you
think, 'I want no one to have any of this.'

He who is happy has a gift for the world.

It is because the world is so full of suffering, that
   your happiness is a gift.
It is because the world is so full of poverty, that
   your wealth is a gift.
It is because the world is so unfriendly, that
   your smile is a gift.
It is because the world is so full of war, that
   your peace of mind is a gift.
It is because the world is in such despair, that
   your hope and optimism are a gift.
It is because the world is so afraid, that
   your love is a gift.

The 'key' to happiness is that *there is no key!*
This might sound like bad news, but fear not!
The good news is that there is no prison,
no door and no lock.
Happiness is open all hours, and if you
are willing to be open to happiness,
you can enjoy happiness *NOW!*

My challenge to you is this:
Do not seek love today; merely be loving.
Do not seek peace today; merely be peaceful.
Do not seek joy today; merely be joyful.
I know it sounds too simple, too silly,
too crazy – but it might just work.
Maybe you really can just be *happy*.

ROBERT HOLDEN

Happiness Now!

Timeless Wisdom for Feeling Good FAST

'I love this book! If you want to embrace a more
powerful and fulfilling way of being in this world,
then immerse yourself in *Happiness Now!*'
Susan Jeffers

'In a world filled with ghastly suffering and sorrow,
Robert Holden's book *Happiness Now!* is a reservoir of
deep nurturing joy ... I consider this book a true gift'
John Bradshaw, author of *Creating Love*

Happiness Now! is a truly powerful journey of exploration
and insight into one of life's most treasured goals. It offers a
message of profound hope and healing. Robert Holden gives
a hugely personal, warm and entertaining account of the
key insights and experiences that led him to develop his
pioneering work into happiness, love and success. Radical
and compassionate, challenging and helpful, visionary and
practical, *Happiness Now!* shows the keys to emotional healing,
true self-acceptance, loving relationship, inner confidence, and
pure peace of mind.

HODDER AND STOUGHTON PAPERBACKS